PARIS 2013

THE CITY AT A GLANCE

Basilique du Sacré-Coeur
Even if you don't venture inside Paul Ab...
postcard staple, the ascent to Sacré-Co...
worth it for the views back across Paris
35 rue du Chevalier-de-la-Barre, 18ᵉ,
T 5341 8900

Palais de Chaillot
This vast neoclassical complex facing the...
Tower was built for the 1937 World's Fair.
1 place du Trocadéro, 16ᵉ, T 5851 5200

Musée du quai Branly
Browse the collection of art from Africa, Asia,
Oceania and the Americas at this arresting
museum designed by architect Jean Nouvel.
See p035

Centre Pompidou
You may need to make several trips here to
take in all that it has to offer, from the iconic
architecture to its world-class exhibitions.
See p014

Maison de Radio France
Henry Bernard's distinctive, aluminium-
plated circular home for the public-service
broadcaster was inaugurated in 1963. It's
currently undergoing renovation.
116 avenue du Président Kennedy, 16ᵉ

Institut du Monde Arabe
Middle Eastern motifs meet Jean Nouvel's
modern architecture in this striking building,
the best of Mitterrand's *Grands Projets*.
1 rue des Fossés Saint-Bernard/Place
Mohammed V, 5ᵉ, T 4051 3838

Tour Montparnasse
Looming over low-rise Paris, this 210m-
high 1970s landmark is back in fashion.
See p010

INTRODUCTION
THE CHANGING FACE OF THE URBAN SCENE

It is tempting to think that Paris never changes, that there is always a corner of the city where you really can catch a glimpse of Eugène de Rastignac, or stumble across a beatific Miles Davis en route to Club Saint-Germain. The truth is, like any other digital-age capital, Paris has become fast-moving and given to trends, even if the insouciant manner of its natives suggests otherwise. Montmartre, so recently fashionable, has settled into a gentrified calm, although it is still a dream for Anglo-Saxons. The *branché* districts right now are the Haut-Marais, where it bleeds into the 10th and 11th arrondissements, and the post-seedy Rue du Faubourg Saint-Denis. That said, visit frequently and you may want to retire from the bobo bustle to enjoy more tranquil areas like the 5th and the leafy 7th. Equally good for slowing the pace, and indulging in some unabashed escapism, are the city's fashion flagships and elite restaurants. Art lovers have it all, from the bourgeois galleries cramming Saint-Germain to acclaimed museums such as Centre Pompidou (see p014) and Palais de Tokyo (see p034).

Plans for Le Grand Paris, a massively ambitious extension of the tightly belted core, will see more change here than at any time since Haussmann, with large-scale urban projects undertaken and the heart of the metropolis redesignated as one of several centres. For now, while you can still walk from the Eiffel Tower to Place de la Bastille and feel you've seen this elegant city, classic Paris lives.

ESSENTIAL INFO
FACTS, FIGURES AND USEFUL ADDRESSES

TOURIST OFFICE
25 rue des Pyramides, 1er
www.parisinfo.com

TRANSPORT
Car hire
Avis
T 4359 0383
www.avis.com
Metro
www.ratp.fr
Trains run from 5.30am until 1am,
Sunday to Thursday; and from 5.30am
until 2am on Fridays and Saturdays
Taxis
Taxis G7
T 4739 4739
Cabs can be hailed in the street or from
ranks at stations and in nightlife districts

EMERGENCY SERVICES
Ambulance
T 15
Fire
T 18
Police
T 17
24-hour pharmacy
Pharmacie Les Champs Dhéry
84 avenue des Champs-Élysées, 8e
T 4562 0241
Open seven days a week

EMBASSIES
British Embassy
35 rue du Faubourg Saint-Honoré, 8e
T 4451 3100
www.ukinfrance.fco.gov.uk
US Embassy
2 avenue Gabriel, 8e
T 4312 2222
france.usembassy.gov

POSTAL SERVICES
Post office
52 rue du Louvre, 1er
T 4028 2151
Shipping
UPS
T 08 2123 3877
www.ups.com

BOOKS
L'Architecture des Années 30 à Paris
by Jean-Marc Larbodière (Charles Massin)
Paris 2000+: New Architecture
by Sam Lubell (Monacelli Press)

WEBSITES
Art/Design
www.designparis.com
www.musee-orsay.fr
Newspaper
www.lemonde.fr

EVENTS
Art Paris
www.artparis.fr
Maison & Objet
www.maison-objet.com
Nuit Blanche
www.nuitblanche.paris.fr

COST OF LIVING
**Taxi from Charles de Gaulle Airport
to city centre**
€50
Cappuccino
€3
Packet of cigarettes
€6
Daily newspaper
€2
Bottle of champagne
€80

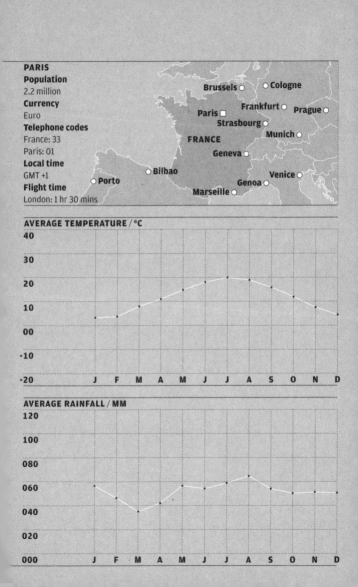

PARIS
Population
2.2 million
Currency
Euro
Telephone codes
France: 33
Paris: 01
Local time
GMT +1
Flight time
London: 1 hr 30 mins

Brussels ○   ○ Cologne
Frankfurt ○   Prague ○
Paris □
Strasbourg ○
Munich ○
FRANCE
Geneva ○
○ Bilbao   Venice ○
○ Porto   Genoa ○
Marseille ○

AVERAGE TEMPERATURE / °C

40											
30											
20											
10											
00											
-10											
-20	J	F	M	A	M	J	J	A	S	O	N	D

AVERAGE RAINFALL / MM

120											
100											
080											
060											
040											
020											
000	J	F	M	A	M	J	J	A	S	O	N	D

NEIGHBOURHOODS

THE AREAS YOU NEED TO KNOW AND WHY

To help you navigate the city, we've chosen the most interesting districts (see below and the map inside the back cover) and colour-coded our featured venues, according to their location; those venues that are outside these areas are not coloured.

MONTMARTRE

Rising above the city, Montmartre remains aloof from the rest of Paris. Check into the tranquil hideaway Hôtel Particulier (see p030) and explore the cafés and *bistrots* on Rue des Martyrs. Make a reservation for dinner at the tiny but top-drawer Guilo Guilo (8 rue Garreau, 18e, T 4254 2392).

CANAL SAINT-MARTIN

It is alongside the banks of this canal that the east-Paris bobo (*bourgeois-bohème*) crowd lingers, weather permitting. Hip Rue Beaurepaire is the epicentre. Stay at Le Citizen Hotel (see p022), where rooms boast canal views. To the east, in the 19th, the bobos continue to push into Belleville.

CHAMPS-ÉLYSÉES

There is a slight stain of tackiness around the Champs-Élysées itself, but the area has much to offer, including aristocratic restaurant Apicius (see p048), and modern luxury hotels such as La Maison Champs Élysées (see p018) and Le Royal Monceau (see p020), revamped by Philippe Starck.

RÉPUBLIQUE/BASTILLE

Rue Oberkampf's legendary nightlife is not what it was, but the area has scrubbed up nicely, with bars such as Aux Deux Amis (No 45, 11e, T 5830 3813) attracting a savvy crowd. Star chef Iñaki Aizpitarte has created a mini monopoly here, thanks to his restaurants Le Dauphin (see p054) and Le Châteaubriand (see p055).

MARAIS

Peppered with galleries and boutiques, the old Jewish quarter centres on Rue des Rosiers, Rue Sainte-Croix de la Bretonnerie and Rue Vieille du Temple. On the eastern border is the fabulous Merci (see p083). Boutique hotel Jules et Jim (see p027) is stylish, affordable and friendly.

BEAUBOURG/LOUVRE

The Louvre (Place du Carrousel, T 4020 5050) is a must, despite its spirit-sapping vastness and the Dan Brown-devouring hordes. Don't miss the Musée des Arts Décoratifs (107 rue de Rivoli, 1er, T 4455 5750), followed by lunch at *néo-bistrot* Spring (6 rue Bailleul, 1er, T 4596 0572).

SAINT-GERMAIN/QUARTIER LATIN

This chic neighbourhood is packed with galleries, cafés and shops, including swish department store Le Bon Marché (24 rue de Sèvres, 7e, T 4439 8000) and the high-design Hermès store (see p078). Further to the east along the river, Les Docks (see p066) is a new creative hub.

LES INVALIDES

Already lined with imposing monuments, this district now boasts Jean Nouvel's Musée du quai Branly (see p035); compare and contrast with the quarter's former highpoint, the UNESCO Headquarters (see p012). Feast and sleep at Thoumieux (see p021), Jean-François Piège's brasserie, restaurant and boutique hotel.

LANDMARKS

THE SHAPE OF THE CITY SKYLINE

Unlike Rome or Venice, Paris never has to live off its past for very long, because it always manages to reinvent itself. How it does this has a lot to do with the structure of the place. Paris has stuck to the same shape for centuries by spreading out steadily from the tiny island, now the Île de la Cité, where the Parisii, a community of Celtic fisherfolk, settled in 250BC. As its population grew, the city expanded outwards in concentric circles, stretching as far as the Périphérique ring road. Chloé-clad commuters lead *Desperate Housewives*-on-the-Seine lifestyles in the leafy western suburbs, such as Saint-Cloud and Neuilly, while the underclass re-enacts *La Haine* in 1950s hellholes north of the ring road.

Contemporary Paris consists of some two million people living inside the 9.7km diameter of the Périphérique, with the Île de la Cité still at its centre. The good news is that, whereas sprawling cities such as Los Angeles can afford to neglect their architecture, land is so precious within the unofficial boundary of Paris that Parisians strive to preserve theirs. And the city puts almost as much effort into building new monuments as it does into cherishing its old ones. Think of Henri IV ordering the construction of an expensive new residential district, the Marais, around Place des Vosges in the early 1600s. All of which means that not only is navigation easy in Paris, but the landmarks that line the way are worth lingering over. *For full addresses, see Resources.*

Tour Montparnasse

The redevelopment of the down-at-heel area around Gare Montparnasse in the early 1960s was, by and large, a piece of inspired city planning. Jean Dubuisson's scheme included a monumental slab of a residential block, with a wonderful gridded curtain wall. Unfortunately, it also allowed for this 210m-high totem pole stuck in the middle of low-rise Paris. Together with the high-rise buildings along the Seine, which were commissioned under the prime ministership of Georges Pompidou, this tower, finished in 1973, is now back in vogue with city opinion-formers. There is an observation terrace, a champagne bar and a glam restaurant, Ciel de Paris, which was designed by Noé Duchaufour-Lawrance, on the 56th floor. *33 avenue du Maine, 15e, T 4538 5256, www.tourmontparnasse56.com*

Grande Arche de la Défense

The proposal to construct a new business district to the west of Paris was first advanced in the early 1950s, but it was this 1989 landmark that fixed La Défense in the popular imagination. A hollowed-out cube standing 110m high, the stark, almost graphic lines of its facades are emphasised by the use of glazing and white Carrara marble. The creation of a Danish duo, architect Johann Otto von Spreckelsen and engineer Erik Reitzel, the arch is scaled on both sides by lifts, providing panoramas of greater Paris, as well as down the axis of the Champs-Élysées (sadly the roof is currently closed to the public). Nearby is Christian de Portzamparc's angular tower for Groupe Société Générale, completed in 2008. *1 parvis de la Défense, T 4907 2727, www.grandearche.com*

UNESCO Headquarters

When this complex was finished in 1958, writer Lewis Mumford dismissed it as a 'museum of antiquated modernities'. Even now, in the eyes of some critics, the building hasn't really recovered from this withering assessment. The work of a trio of celebrated architects, Marcel Breuer, Pier Luigi Nervi and Bernard Zehrfuss, it was one of the first major modern works to be constructed in the centre of the city. All the same, the seven-storey, Y-shaped office building (left), resting on 72 concrete stilts, has become a landmark, and the congress hall, with its concertina-like structure, has come to be seen as a masterpiece of modern design. Picasso, Miró, Tàpies and Le Corbusier were some of the artists commissioned to create works for the complex. In 1995, Japanese architect Tadao Ando added an exquisite small meditation space to the site.
7 place de Fontenoy, 7ᵉ, www.unesco.org

Centre Pompidou

The moment when architecture became icon can be traced squarely back to 1977, when Richard Rogers and Renzo Piano's technical and functional tour de force was unveiled to the world. One of the most visited venues in France, it can appear a little untidy, but it is the classic example of a building as a city symbol. *Place Georges Pompidou, 4ᵉ, T 4478 1233, www.centrepompidou.fr*

HOTELS

WHERE TO STAY AND WHICH ROOMS TO BOOK

Paris is one of the world's great hotel cities, but nowhere, except perhaps New York, is the dissonance between palatial lobbies and bijoux rooms more jarring. You need the cost/benefit analysis skills of an economist to work out the trade-off between a good *chambre* in a modest hotel and vice versa. If regular visitors used to complain about restricted options, though, now the scene is abuzz.

There are exciting places to stay in edgy, upcoming districts, such as Le Citizen (see p022) by Canal Saint-Martin, and Mama Shelter (see p028) in the 20th arrondissement. To the west, and more luxurious, is La Maison Champs Élysées (see p018), now super-chic following a redesign by Maison Martin Margiela. Two rare 'restaurants with rooms' have opened on opposite sides of the city: the opulent Hôtel Thoumieux (see p021), and the affordable Auberge Flora (44 boulevard Richard-Lenoir, 11e, T 4700 5277), which has interiors by architects Simone&Hug. Less expensive, yet stylish, options are the central Crayon Hôtel (25 rue du Bouloi, 1er, T 4236 5419), and Jules et Jim (see p027).

At the glitzier end are the Asian brands now resident in Paris, including the Mandarin Oriental (247-251 rue Saint-Honoré, 1er, T 7098 7888) and The Peninsula (19 avenue Kléber), due to take reservations in 2013. W Paris Opéra (4 rue Meyerbeer, 9e, T 7748 9494) is a fashionable choice across the road from Palais Garnier. *For full addresses and room rates, see Resources.*

La Réserve

Set in a belle époque townhouse on the Place du Trocadéro, La Réserve feels less like a hotel and more like a private residence. Designed by Rémi Tessier, who is well known for his work on yacht interiors, this luxurious property has an understated decor, screening rooms and private gardens. What the hotel lacks in amenities (there's no room service or gym), it makes up for with other attributes: staff prepare breakfast in your kitchen each morning, and no request is too challenging for the resident concierge. Of the 10 accommodations, we suggest Apartments 1 (the largest), 3 or 5, which all have panoramic views of the Eiffel Tower. La Réserve is well placed for visiting Palais de Tokyo (see p034). *10 place du Trocadéro, 16ᵉ, T 5370 5370, www.lareserve-paris.com*

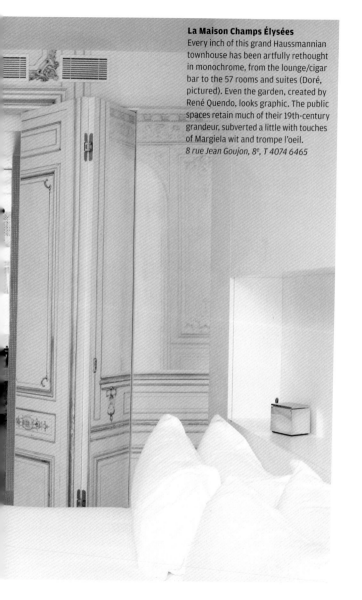

La Maison Champs Élysées

Every inch of this grand Haussmannian townhouse has been artfully rethought in monochrome, from the lounge/cigar bar to the 57 rooms and suites (Doré, pictured). Even the garden, created by René Quendo, looks graphic. The public spaces retain much of their 19th-century grandeur, subverted a little with touches of Margiela wit and trompe l'oeil.
8 rue Jean Goujon, 8ᵉ, T 4074 6465

Le Royal Monceau

Established in 1928 and reopened in 2010 after a major overhaul by Philippe Starck, this plush hotel is packed with art. You will spot an installation (a giant teapot) by Joana Vasconcelos in the garden, and Stéphane Calais' fresco in the in-house French restaurant, La Cuisine. Aspiring . collectors will be encouraged to learn that the majority of works on display are for sale, and that there is a small art gallery within the hotel. We recommend checking into one of the spacious Gallery Suites, each of which has a unique decor. Browse in the art bookshop and stroll through the garden, which was designed by *paysagiste* Louis Benech. There's also a screening room, Le Cinéma des Lumières, which is used for film festivals and premieres. *37 avenue Hoche, 8e, T 4299 8800, www.leroyalmonceau.com*

Hôtel Thoumieux

One of the smartest addresses you will bag in Paris for less than €300 a night, this boutique residence is distinguished by its lavish interior design, courtesy of India Mahdavi, and its pair of destination restaurants. Chef Jean-François Piège, formerly at Hôtel de Crillon, opened a brasserie (see p056) here in 2009; a gastronomic restaurant (agleam with two Michelin stars) followed a year later, then the hotel in 2011. In the 15 sumptuous rooms, including one suite (above), every detail, from the key fob to the bathrobes, is a pleasure to look at and to handle. The restaurant does an exquisite tasting menu, and the brasserie, where breakfast is served, offers a terrific snapshot of the tony 7th and its well-shod habitués.
79 rue Saint-Dominique, 7ᵉ, T 4705 4975, www.thoumieux.fr

Le Citizen Hotel

It's as if the bobos of Saint-Martin dreamed up this hotel. Opened in 2010, Le Citizen is a subtle exercise in urban cool, thanks to architects Christophe Delcourt and Stéphane Lanchon. All 12 rooms have canal views; our pick is Zen Suite 66 (pictured). The iPads issued to guests come loaded with itinerary tips. *96 quai de Jemmapes, 10ᵉ, T 8362 5550, www.lecitizenhotel.com*

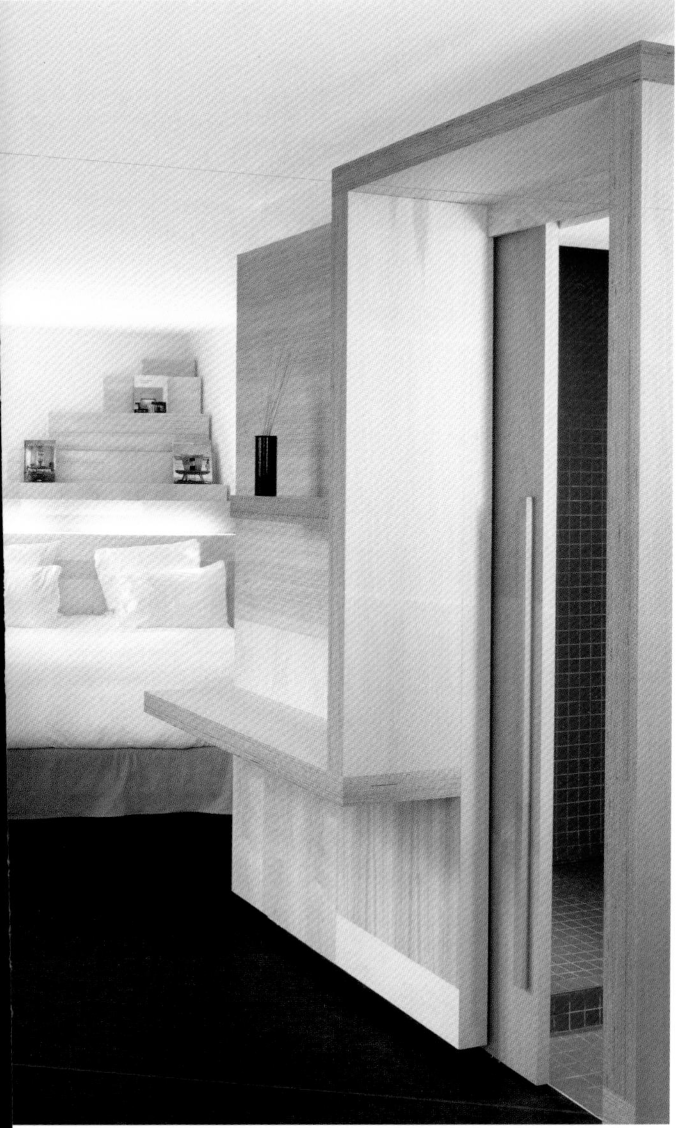

Le Pavillon de la Reine

Unequivocally the finest hotel in the Marais, Le Pavillon de la Reine resides on the handsome Place des Vosges. Following an extensive refurbishment between 2010 and 2012, under the direction of Didier Benderli of Kérylos Intérieurs, the hotel emerged as a curious mix of the old (four-poster beds, exposed beams) and new – the interiors are classically modern rather than contemporary. Reserve a Superior Room overlooking the courtyard or, if money is no object, the Suite de la Reine (above). Parisians talk about this place as if it were a secret. The word has definitely spread about its small yet outstanding spa, which is run by Carita and incorporates a gym, a jacuzzi and a steam bath. *28 place des Vosges, 3e, T 4029 1919, www.pavillon-de-la-reine.com*

3 Rooms

After creating the Milan jewel 10 Corso Como, Carla Sozzani got together with Tunisian-born fashion designer Azzedine Alaïa to open a small hotel in Paris. The three apartments are a study in understated perfection. Alaïa donated furniture from his private collection, including chairs by Marc Newson and tables by Jean Prouvé. Each apartment is self-contained, two come with ample double bedrooms, and the third (above) has two bedrooms and sleeps three (the rates increase according to the number of guests). The location, on a peaceful street in the Marais, is just steps away from Alaïa's atelier and his boutique at 7 rue de Moussy (T 4272 1919), which was designed by Marc Newson in collaboration with architect Sébastien Segers.

5 rue de Moussy, 4e, T 4478 9200

bar >
02 >
15/16/17 >

Hôtel Jules et Jim

Built virtually from scratch on the site of an old precious-metal workshop, Jules et Jim is modish but not overweeningly trendy; it has its arty moments and a pretty cool bar, but is an affordable and friendly base for everyone. The five-year conversion, undertaken with architect Heinrich Fitger and interior designers Atome Associés, has been a labour of love for the owners, Geoffroy Sciard and Antoine Brault. There are four styles of room, including diminutive pods with glowing bauxite walls and rooftop views, and more neutral rooms in a second building. Drinks and breakfast are served in the former carriage house, decorated with 1950s-style tables, settees from Red Edition and chairs by local firm Anégil. *11 rue des Gravilliers, 3e, T 4454 1313, www.hoteljulesetjim.com*

Mama Shelter
It's a schlep from the centre, but this is one of the most interesting places to stay in Paris. Carved out of a former multistorey car park, it was conceived as a witty hotel-cum-urban-retreat by Serge Trigano + Sons, Cyril Aouizerate, Philippe Starck and Roland Castro. Stay in Room 526 (pictured) and hang out in the lobby/bar/restaurant.
109 rue de Bagnolet, 20e, T 4348 4848

Hôtel Particulier Montmartre

Despite the swarms of tourists en route to Sacré-Coeur, and slow but steady gentrification, pockets of the Montmartre district retain an atmosphere unmatched anywhere else in Paris. Walk north of Place des Abbesses to the stylish Avenue Junot to arrive at the discreetly situated Hôtel Particulier. Spread across a 19th-century townhouse, once owned by the Hermès family, it looks on to private gardens by Louis Benech. The property was transformed into a five-suite hotel by filmmaker Morgane Rousseau, who decorated the rooms, adding works by French artists. Reserve the monochrome Poèmes et Chapeaux (opposite) or Rideau de Cheveux Suite, which features portrait photography by Natacha Lesueur.
23 avenue Junot, 18e, T 5341 8140, www.hotel-particulier-montmartre.com

24 HOURS
SEE THE BEST OF THE CITY IN JUST ONE DAY

We all have our fantasies of the perfect Parisian day. Owing to its petite size relative to London, say, or New York, this city smiles on visitors who want to explore both sides of the Seine. Start your day at the top, on Rue des Martyrs, the gourmet street that winds down from Montmartre; if you continue south along Rue du Faubourg Montmartre, there's plenty more food shopping around Montorgueil. Or rent a Vélib (www.velib.paris.fr) and devote your time to contemporary art and design. Tour Palais de Tokyo (see p034), then cross Pont de l'Alma to visit Musée du quai Branly (see p035) A memorable lunch can be had nearby at Stéphane Jégo's Chez l'Ami Jean (27 rue Malar, 7ᵉ, T 4705 8689) or tapas bar Bellota-Bellota (18 rue Jean-Nicot, 7ᵉ, T 5359 9696). Continue further down the Left Bank to the Latin Quarter, to browse the exemplary Galerie Kreo (see p036). From here, switch off with a stroll in Jardin du Luxembourg or Jardin des Plantes, en route to the recently constructed Cité de la Mode et du Design (see p066), situated in the 13th arrondissement along the bank of the Seine.

Begin your evening with a glass of pale-red Jura wine at the earthy Le Baron Rouge (1 rue Théophile Roussel, 12ᵉ, T 4343 1432) near Marché d'Aligre (Place d'Aligre). From here, it's an easy stroll to dinner at the hip, youthful Septime (see p038) or Rino (46 rue Trousseau, 11ᵉ, T 4806 9585; open Tuesday to Saturday).
For full addresses, see Resources.

10.30 Pâtisserie des Martyrs

A new destination for *lèche-vitrine* on Rue des Martyrs, this gleaming boutique is far more than a pâtisserie: it's a showcase for the *friandises*, viennoiseries and cakes of a perfectionist. Son of a famed Lorraine *boulanger*, Sébastien Gaudard trained with Pierre Hermé and was top gun at Fauchon aged only 26; this is his debut solo venture. Beyond the shop's racing-green frontage, the interior is akin to a doll's house, all polished glass cases, bell jars, shelves of confectionery, and just-right *macarons*, millefeuilles and tarts. (The pâtisserie is closed on Mondays.) Coffee connoisseurs should walk up the road to Kooka Boora Café Shop (T 5692 1241); if tea and toast are more your style, Rose Bakery (T 4282 1280) opens at 9am for breakfast. *22 rue des Martyrs, 9ᵉ, T 7118 2470, www.sebastiengaudard.com*

12.00 Palais de Tokyo

Recently extended, this venue is a must, for its surveys of contemporary art and its architecture – a 22,000 sq m labyrinth of white walls, lofty alcoves and concrete chambers. Architects Anne Lacaton and Jean-Philippe Vassal took a minimalist approach to the renovation, freeing up space and revealing the building's vast proportions. In some of the rooms, it can feel as if you're entering a no-go area, so unsignposted and unrefined is the finish. As many of the artworks are disruptive of normative seeing and thinking, the experience can be thrillingly disorienting. The programme rotates three times a year, and the venue's fabric is also subject to artistic intervention. The museum opens at noon and is closed on Tuesdays.
*13 avenue du Président Wilson, 16ᵉ,
T 8197 3588, www.palaisdetokyo.com*

13.00 Musée du quai Branly

In 2008, French architect Jean Nouvel finally picked up his Pritzker. Long overdue, perhaps, although his friend Frank Gehry was quick to offer an explanation. Unlike Zaha Hadid, or Gehry himself, Nouvel has no signature style. His projects are site-specific attempts at unique buildings. The 1987 Institut du Monde Arabe (T 4051 3838) made the architect a star. After that came Fondation Cartier (T 4218 5650) in 1994, and then Musée du quai Branly in 2006, which is where to begin your Nouvel tour. Exhibiting non-Western art, the building resembles a long footbridge set amid a forest of green. It's protected from the Quai Branly traffic by a glass screen, and a vertical garden designed by Patrick Blanc covers one of the walls. *37 quai Branly, 7e, T 5661 7000, www.quaibranly.fr*

16.00 Galerie Kreo

Seeing itself as something of a 'research laboratory', Galerie Kreo is devoted to artistic exploration in design. Opened in 1999 by Clémence and Didier Krzentowski, it has secured exclusive international rights to an impressive selection of limited-edition furniture, objects and lighting by such renowned creatives as Jasper Morrison, Martin Szekely and Wieki Somers. The Krzentowskis have a fluid arrangement with designers, accepting that development takes time and money. Their particular expertise in contemporary design-art has led to a roster of superior exhibitions, such as 'Techniques Mixtes et Dimensions Variables' (left), which showed Alessandro Mendini's 'Tabouret Enigma', Hella Jongerius' 'Swatch' table, Ronan & Erwan Bouroullec's 'Objets Lumineux' and Pierre Charpin's 'Ignotus Nomen' vase.
31 rue Dauphine, 6ᵉ, T 5310 2300, www.galeriekreo.com

20.00 Septime

This low-key yet buzzy dining room near Bastille serves brilliant *bistronomique* cuisine. Once you've taken your seat amid the rustic/industrial decor, simply request 'red' or 'white' for an *apéro*, divulge any food intolerances, and the rest is decided for you. Chef Bertrand Grébaut's €55 carte blanche menu makes the most of what's in season: that could be cod with asparagus and grilled nasturtium leaves; duck with yellow beetroot; and modish desserts that avoid pastry and cream. The food is refined and the crowd is elegant too, with more chic suits than hip scruffs. Attentive staff ensure the vibe is never too laidback. Grébaut formerly cooked at L'Arpège with Alain Passard, a 'natural' chef who inspired Noma and the New Nordics.
80 rue de Charonne, 11ᵉ, T 4367 3829, www.septime-charonne.fr

URBAN LIFE

CAFÉS, RESTAURANTS, BARS AND NIGHTCLUBS

The *bistronomie* scene that restored the city's culinary verve is well established now, and Septime (see p038), Le Châteaubriand (see p055) and Frenchie (see p058) supply some of the most dynamic dining in Paris. Newcomers like L'Office (see p044) and Neva Cuisine (2 rue de Berne, 8ᵉ, T 4522 1891) are easing off the New Nordic style and no-choice menus, but maintaining the buzzy informality. Pascal Barbot's L'Astrance (4 rue Beethoven, 16ᵉ, T 4050 8440) is where British chefs glean cutting-edge ideas from the Asian-influenced menu. For something earthier and less pricey, Chez L'Ami Jean (see p032) is a former Basque stalwart in the 7th where you can eat like a king. The *bistrot* to end them all is Paul Bert (18 rue Paul Bert, 11ᵉ, T 4372 2401), which has a seafood sibling, L'Ecailler du Bistrot (T 4372 7677), nearby at No 22.

The trend for casual dining, and a fastidiousness about *terroir*, mean that wine bars are having a prolonged moment. Bobos like Aux Deux Amis (45 rue Oberkampf, 11ᵉ, T 5830 3813) for natural wines, while Verjus (47 rue Montpensier, 1ᵉʳ, T 4297 5440) offers adroit tasting menus. Albion (80 rue du Faubourg Poissonnière, 10ᵉ, T 4246 0244) is more of a *bistrot* but is aimed at oenophiles. Later in the evening, head to Candelaria (52 rue de Saintonge, 3ᵉ) or swankier Le 29 (29 rue Vineuse, 8ᵉ) for cocktails. Nightclubwise, Le Baron (6 avenue Marceau, 8ᵉ) has definitely still got it. *For full addresses, see Resources.*

L'Opéra

For once, a genuinely 'long-awaited' new restaurant. More than 135 years after the ornate Palais Garnier was completed, Odile Decq's L'Opéra has transformed an underused corner of the 19th-century landmark, giving show-goers a smart place to eat and drink, and attracting execs and Galerie Lafayette pilgrims too. The space behind the eastern facade's pillars is now replete with a curvaceous red-and-white mezzanine (above), which overhangs a red-carpeted ground-floor area. The new interior is engineered in steel, aluminium, wood and glass. The menu is high-end: poached and roasted chicken supreme with morels and lovage shoots; pata negra pork with honey, elderberry, polenta and olive emulsion. The bar serves proper martinis. *Palais Garnier, Place Jacques Roucher, 9ᵉ, T 4268 8680, www.opera-restaurant.fr*

Le Bal Café

Housed in a former ballroom, Le Bal opened in 2010 as an exhibition space focusing on photography, film and new media. It includes a bookshop and a café, where the menu is as accomplished as any of the arts projects. There are non-Gallic entries on the menu, such as potted mackerel, and Gubbeen cheese.
*6 impasse de la Défense, 17ᵉ,
T 4470 7551, www.le-bal.fr*

L'Office

Not as avowedly *bistronomique* as some of the chef-owned newcomers to the Paris scene, L'Office is nonetheless on-trend with its market-led blackboard menu and good-value *formules*, from €21 at lunch and €27 at dinner. *Cochon, borlotti, scarole* is pork and beans, but elegantly done: loin and smoky confit shoulder with escarole leaves and puréed borlotti. A recent change of chef should not affect this bistro – the young yet experienced owner/sommelier Charles Compagnon is in charge here. He designed the interior with his friend, architect Vincent Eschalier, choosing dark tables and flooring, green and grey walls, and lighting from filament bulbs on draped red flex. Mark-ups on the mainly *bio*, well-balanced wines are fair, and the Ethiopian Yirgacheffe coffee is remarkable.
3 rue Richer, 9e, T 4770 6731

Compagnie des Vins Surnaturels
This civilised evening hangout is a bit of
a tease, namewise. The 400-bin wine list
leans away from low-sulphite *vins naturels*;
in fact, the foremost wine expert among
the owners is a big Bordeaux dealer.
Well-heeled thirty- and fortysomething
Parisians saunter in here after work,
settling into upholstered armchairs and
ikat-print sofas chosen by young French
designer Dorothée Meilichzon, and
spending from €20 to several hundred
euros on Bordeaux reds, whites from
Burgundy and the Loire, and interesting
cuvées from the south, Italy, even Israel
and Uruguay. Good entry-level wines
include Louis Jadot Couvent des Jacobins
Bourgogne, and Laporte Terre des Anges
Sancerre. The food is secondary, with
bellota ham or a cheese platter advised
over the fancier-sounding propositions.
7 rue Lobineau, 6ᵉ, T 954 902 020,
www.compagniedesvinssurnaturels.com

Apicius

Almost everything you read about Apicius makes Jean-Pierre Vigato's temple to fine dining sound faintly ridiculous. His use of Heinz tomato ketchup in delicate fish dishes, or the overpowering sweet-and-sour sauce he makes for the finest, most delicate foie gras. In short, none of it should work; in practice, almost all of it does. If there is a fault, it is that we are solidly in gastro-tourism territory here, and the clientele can veer away from the glamorous in the direction of the over-earnest – although the space offers the necessary sense of occasion, and the food really is sensational enough to convert even the terminally jaded. Be sure to call ahead, as the restaurant is closed at the weekend and throughout August. *20 rue d'Artois, 8ᵉ, T 4380 1966, www.restaurant-apicius.com*

La Villa

Boasting a piano lounge and views to the Arc de Triomphe, this is the spot for an alfresco lunch or stylish dinner and drinks. Designed by Dorothée Boissier and Patrick Gilles, both Philippe Starck disciples and now respected names in their own right, the restaurant is located in a mansion once owned by art dealer Paul Durand-Ruel, who stuffed it with Impressionist works. Taking this as their cue, the duo installed wood panelling, clever lighting and, in the winter garden, a ceiling fresco by Cyprien Chabert, which recalls the art that once hung inside. Sit in a booth and dine on classic French fare (seared beef tartare, rum baba) or a range of other cuisines, or perch at the bar within foot-tapping distance of the Steinway.
37 avenue de Friedland, 8e, T 8228 7508, www.lavilla-paris.com

Sur Mesure par Thierry Marx
Design team Patrick Jouin and Sanjit
Manku's white-on-white restaurant
at the Mandarin Oriental (see p016)
cocoons guests in a space-age polygon.
Chef Thierry Marx, dubbed 'the French
Heston' due to his lab-based research
and ultra-precise modern cuisine, melds
Japanese inspirations with astounding
technique to create light, ludic dishes.
251 rue Saint-Honoré, 1er, T 7098 7300

Le 39V

Situated on the highest floor of a classic Haussmannian building, Le 39V has an arresting interior featuring an angular, shell-like ceiling and a dining room that wraps around an internal courtyard. Created by the Paris-based practice Naço Architectures, the interior design complements the modern brasserie cuisine prepared by chef Frédéric Vardon, a former student of Alain Ducasse. Order an aperitif at the glossy bar (above) before sampling the menu. The two set-lunch options, which change weekly according to the best fresh ingredients available, and the seasonal tasting menu offer the best value. If you arrive in the day, have drinks on the terrace – it's a secret spot in this part of town.
39 avenue George V, 8e, T 5662 3905, www.le39v.com

Le Dauphin

Although technically a wine bar, Le Dauphin has foodies in a spin over its exquisite tapas menu by Iñaki Aizpitarte of Le Châteaubriand fame (T 4357 4595). Knuckle of pork with turnips, white tuna with Sicilian onions and aubergines, and tandoori octopus are just some of his concoctions. These compete with a carefully chosen wine list, including many available at €5 a glass – Aizpitarte is a democrat when it comes to menu pricing. Opened in 2010, Le Dauphin was designed by architect Rem Koolhaas, who installed acres of Carrara marble, mirrors and a large central bar. The perfect Aizpitarte combo? Head here for some drinks and *amuse-bouches* while waiting for the no-reservations-required second sitting (a maximum of four people after 9.30pm) at Le Châteaubriand a few doors down. *131 avenue Parmentier, 11ᵉ, T 5528 7888, www.restaurantledauphin.net*

Brasserie Thoumieux
This venue was relaunched in 2009 by chef Jean-François Piège, formerly of Les Ambassadeurs at Hôtel de Crillon, and Thierry Costes, of the family behind Paris' see-and-be-seen destinations. The menu and the interior have been restored to their former glory, and the staff are equally pleasing to behold. *79 rue Saint-Dominique, 7ᵉ, T 4705 4975, www.thoumieux.com*

Frenchie

The only way to eat here is to find the unmarked door to the tiny dining room, and ask if there's been a cancellation that week. Chef/patron Gregory Marchand admits that it's even hard for his in-laws to get a table. His much-lauded restaurant is a modern take on a traditional Parisian *bistrot*, founded in 2009 when Marchand returned to France after stints at New York's Gramercy Tavern and Jamie Oliver's Fifteen in London. Famed for its market-dictated *bistronomie*, the menu changes daily, although the wines and the hearty cheeseboard remain consistent. Don't fret if you can't get a table – its sibling, Frenchie Bar à Vins (T 4039 9619), on the other side of the street, doesn't take reservations. Both close at the weekend. *5 rue du Nil, 2e, T 4039 9619, www.frenchie-restaurant.com*

Saturne

Chef Sven Chartier, just 24 years old at the time, opened Saturne with sommelier Ewen Lemoigne in 2010. The restaurant's pared-back, Scandinavian-style interior features undressed wooden tables, stone walls and an open kitchen, which are all illuminated by the giant skylight and light fittings by Serge Mouille and Céline Wright. Try the five- or seven-course carte blanche lunch menu, priced at €55 and €69 respectively, or the €60 seven-step dinner, which utilises fresh, impeccably sourced ingredients to produce dishes such as vine stalk and polenta pigeon, and beef, raspberry and nasturtium tartare. The *vins naturels* on the wine list are best negotiated with Lemoigne's guidance. Saturne is closed at the weekend.

17 rue Notre-Dame des Victoires, 2ᵉ, T 4260 3190, www.saturne-paris.fr

Beef Club

Anglo-Saxon trends are giving Paris what for right now: Le Camion Qui Fume (www.lecamionquifume.com), the city's lone food truck, sells out of burgers daily, cheesecake is a hot topic and critics enthuse over Beef Club, the first restaurant from the prolific Experimental Cocktail Club crew. In an ex-butcher's shop by Les Halles, beneath a tin ceiling and exposed brickwork, a young crowd devours €23 burgers garnished with grilled onions, pickles, Ogleshield and Red Leicester. The beef is supplied by Yorkshireman Tim Wilson, owner of the Ginger Pig, but aged under the watchful eye of French artisan butcher Yves-Marie Le Bourdonnec. There's also Scotch egg and macaroni cheese. The basement Ballroom bar serves the likes of Miss You Harry, a blend of bitter chocolate, genmaicha tea and Japanese whisky.
58 rue Jean-Jacques Rousseau, 1ᵉʳ,
T 954 371 365, www.eccbeefclub.com

INSIDER'S GUIDE
JULIE ROUSSELET, FASHION DESIGNER

Founder of Flouzen (www.flouzen.com), a cashmere accessories brand, Paris-born Julie Rousselet now resides near Musée d'Orsay. Her atelier is nearby in Saint-Germain-des-Prés, where she adores the elegant streets and architecture. She heads to the *bio* Marché Raspail (Boulevard Raspail/Rue du Cherche-Midi) every Sunday and enjoys the classic Parisian cafés dotted around. Rousselet is a Left Bank person, although she does cross the river to buy records at Balades Sonores (1 avenue Trudaine, 9e, T 8387 9487).

At breakfast time, Rousselet tips the *pain au chocolat* at Bread & Roses (7 rue Fleurus, 6e, T 4222 0606). A customer of Crêperie des Canettes (10 rue des Canettes, 6e, T 4326 2765) for more than 15 years, she also lunches at Bar de la Croix Rouge (2 carrefour de la Croix Rouge, 6e, T 4548 0645) – mostly a roast beef sandwich on the terrace. If in need of a sweet treat, she'll buy an apple turnover at Pâtisserie des Rêves (93 rue du Bac, 7e, T 4284 0082).

For *apéro*, L'Avant-Comptoir (3 carrefour de l'Odéon, 6e, T 4427 0797) is a busy bar serving wine and charcuterie. Convivial bistro L'Affable (10 rue de Saint-Simon, 7e, T 4222 0160) offers fine *ris de veau*, while the Mont-Blanc dessert at Le Cinq Mars (51 rue de Verneuil, 7e, T 4544 6913) is, she reckons, as good as *crème de marrons* gets. Later on, she appreciates the cocktails and the decor at David Lynch's Silencio (142 rue Montmartre, 2e, T 4013 1233). *For full addresses, see Resources.*

ARCHITOUR
A GUIDE TO THE CITY'S ICONIC BUILDINGS

There are a dozen Le Corbusier buildings in and around Paris, the city where he lived and worked for most of his adult life. Today, some, such as Villa Besnus (85 boulevard de la République), the family home he completed in 1922 in the suburb of Vaucresson, are almost unrecognisable. Others, such as the 1951 Maisons Jaoul (83 rue de Longchamp, 16e) in leafy Neuilly-sur-Seine, which were gossip-magazine staples when they belonged to Lord Palumbo and served as a base for his friends (including Princess Diana), have been carefully restored. Most of Le Corbusier's Paris projects are concentrated in a crescent across the southern half of the city and can be squeezed into half a day's architourism, or combined, as we suggest, with a selection of other modern gems.

Cité de Refuge (12 rue Cantagrel, 13e) is a good start. Nearby is Maison Planeix (24 boulevard Masséna, 13e). A house-cum-studio, it was designed for one of Le Corbu's most ardent, if impecunious, clients, the sculptor Antonin Planeix. Atelier Ozenfant (53 avenue Reille, 14e) is another live/work space by the architect. By the early 1930s, Le Corbusier was back in the 14th for his first public commission, Pavillon Suisse. He revisited the site for Maison du Brésil (71 boulevard Jourdan, 14e, T 5810 2300) in 1959. Fondation Le Corbusier (8-10 square du Docteur Blanche, 16e, T 4288 4153; closed Sundays and Monday morning) can advise on visits.
For full addresses, see Resources.

Maison de Verre

One of the greatest houses built in the International Style is one of the least visited. Architects Pierre Chareau and Bernard Bijvoet, together with metal craftsman Louis Dalbet, worked wonders on the bones of an existing building on a small plot in the 7th arrondissement, completing the new one in 1932. The facades are covered with glass blocks set into a steel frame, which creates a well of light while ensuring privacy. The living room is the real show-stopper. One wall is covered with a sliding-panel bookcase, and features louvres, exposed bolts and thin slabs of slate. Wires were threaded through the metal tubing that runs from floor to ceiling. Visits are severely restricted, alas, but it is possible to glimpse the house from the outside.

31 rue Saint-Guillaume, 7ᵉ

Cité de la Mode et du Design

Vivid pea-green girders and broad decks define Jakob + MacFarlane's contemporary fashion and design centre, recast from a 1907 goods depot. The new carapace is an extension of the riverside promenade and enlivens this historically bleak area, dubbed Les Docks. L'Institut Français de la Mode is at one end and the bar/club/restaurant Wanderlust, run by the Savoir Faire group (Silencio, Social Club) occupies the other. In between are exhibition spaces, cafés and boutiques. An expanse of grass covers the roof, home of the massive 1,100 sq m Moon Roof nightclub. The rest of the building's 'skin' comprises glass and steel. Les Docks is an admirable project. Whether it beds in as a true creative hub, only time will tell.

34 quai d'Austerlitz, 13ᵉ, T 7677 2530, www.paris-docks-en-seine.fr

Communist Party Headquarters

The French Communist Party is blessed with a magnificent seat from which to orchestrate its policies. Designed by architect Oscar Niemeyer (a committed communist), its HQ is one of the city's finest pieces of modernist architecture: an undulating glazed building with a series of subterranean chambers. The highlight is the sculptural conference hall, which has a white domed roof that rises in front of the main structure. Niemeyer collaborated with Jean Prouvé on the sinuous glass curtain wall and its mechanical window openers, and designed the furniture. Tours can be arranged by appointment, or you may be invited to an event here – Prada once rented the building for a show.
2 place du Colonel Fabien, 10ᵉ,
T 4040 1212

Boulogne-Billancourt

Unless there is a special place in your heart reserved for hotbeds of 1960s radicalism, it is unlikely that the grimy, still rather edgy *banlieue* of Boulogne-Billancourt will have featured heavily in your trips to Paris. But the site of the Renault strikes of 1968 is a surprisingly good place to search out overlooked architectural gems, such as Le Corbusier's early Maison Cook, Maison Collinet by Robert Mallet-Stevens, and the liner-like apartments built by Georges-Henri Pingusson in 1936 – all located on Rue Denfert-Rochereau. Although these buildings take some tracking down, it is impossible to miss the suburb's more recent claim to architectural fame – the mid-1970s city of apartments (pictured), by Daniel Badani, Pierre Roux-Dorlut and Pierre Vigneron, which reshaped the skyline along Rue de Vieux Pont de Sèvres.

SHOPPING
THE BEST RETAIL THERAPY AND WHAT TO BUY

The concept store was arguably conceived in Paris, and the Colette effect is still evident among independent boutiques and big-brand stores alike. Designed by Federico Masotto, Surface to Air (108 rue Vieille du Temple, 3e, T 4461 7627) showcases the multifaceted label's fashion lines, as well as its art and design projects. Galerie BSL (see p084) turns shopping into an art form by offering design and jewellery in a gallery space, and at Merci (see p083), vintage wares are sold alongside clothes and home accessories.

At the grand fashion houses, radical architecture is de rigueur. In 2010, Balenciaga (10 avenue George V, 8e, T 4720 2111) unveiled a spacecraft-like flagship designed by creative director Nicolas Ghesquière and artist Dominique Gonzalez-Foerster. For its first store on the Rive Gauche, Hermès (see p078) employed RDAI to construct striking installations. Reincarnated leather-goods brand Moynat (see p079) also has a sleek home for its finely crafted bags.

Lifestyle stores offering bespoke services to younger Parisians are opening, marking a return to specialisation: Nose (see p089) is a fragrance store with savvy advisers; En Selle Marcel (see p074) caters to the cycling cognoscenti. At Boutique des Saveurs (61 rue du Faubourg Saint-Denis, 10e, T 4770 4469), Lucien Olivo and Franck Altruie fill the shelves of their reinvented *épicerie* with comestibles from all over France's regional natural parks.
For full addresses, see Resources.

Cousu de Fil Blanc

Made in France, this new range of pure, paraben-free vegetable soaps has been formulated with non-floral scents and premium ingredients. The White Collection follows a milky theme: Lait de Montagne has a honeyed alpine fragrance, and Lait d'Amandes' almond milk formula is for sensitive skin. Spicy Coffee, Seaweed and Black Tea (above, top), €10 per 100g, are the Black Collection's vital elements, and Collection Réhab's 3% Miel Bio bar (above), €10 per 100g, contains organic chestnut honey. The brains behind the brand is Carole Dichampt, a textile designer with a nose for a therapeutic fragrance, a yen for healing plants and an eye for exquisite packaging. Buy the soaps at Khadi & Co (T 4274 7132), Colette (T 5535 3390) and Bon Marché Rive Gauche (T 4439 8000). *www.cousudefilblanc.com*

En Selle Marcel

Cycling is super-cool in Paris right now. Located between the foodie Montorgueil quarter and hip Saint-Denis, the brilliantly named En Selle Marcel ('On yer bike, Marcel') is a boutique that caters not just for style-conscious-yet-wobbly Pashley types, but serious cycling connoisseurs. Vintage bikes by Raleigh and Peugeot are parked up for drooling over, Cinelli frames hang on the wall, and new breeds include Bianchi fixies and ABICI 1950s-inspired designs. Rapha and Brooks are partner brands; there's clothing from Misericordia, hard-wearing manbags made by Jojo Messenger, and ABICI helmets disguised as natty green loden caps. At the rear is a workshop, but you won't see a spot of grease on the shop's painted grey floor.
40 rue Tiquetonne, 2ᵉ, T 4454 0646, www.ensellemarcel.over-blog.com

Naço Gallery

In the south-east of the city, this gallery is an offshoot of the multidisciplinary Naço architectural firm, which was founded by the Argentina-born Marcelo Joulia. Naço's commitment to global practice extends from the international work of its offices in Paris, Shanghai and Buenos Aires, to this gallery just off Rue du Faubourg Saint-Antoine, which showcases a roster of artists from different creative fields.

Previous exhibitions have included the photography of Daniel Tubío, Marcos Lopez and Amir Anoushfar. A display of works (above) by Monobloque, a young Berlin-based collective which explores the relationship between graphics, the design of objects and architecture, exemplifies the gallery's pioneering approach.
38 rue de Citeaux, 12ᵉ, T 4345 0666, www.nacogallery.wordpress.com

Atelier 154

Tucked down a cobblestoned mews in the northern part of République, Stéphane Quatresous' design gallery and workshop is a source of vintage furnishings and lighting, as well as the creations of its founder. Quatresous' industrial-influenced furniture includes clean-lined tables and robust storage units, all made to order from steel.
154 rue Oberkampf, 11ᵉ

Hermès Sèvres

After restoring this 1935 art deco indoor swimming pool, Hermès turned to Rena Dumas Architecture Interieure (RDAI) to embellish the fashion brand's first concept boutique. Three tall, undulating 'teepees', constructed from woven ash, rise 9m above a floor that shimmers with original mosaics and functions as the main retail space. A fourth structure sits on the staircase that leads from the entrance level and overlooks the spectacle, its wrought-iron balconies echoing those at the Hermès HQ on Rue du Faubourg Saint-Honoré. Visit the Le Plongeoir tearoom, the in-house florist Baptiste Pitou (T 4284 1908) and the Chaine d'Encre bookstore (T 4284 4157), before perusing the entire range of Hermès fashion and homewares. *17 rue de Sèvres, 6e, T 4222 8083, www.hermes.com*

Moynat

Competing nobly with the big guns of *haute maroquinerie*, Moynat reopened shop on Rue Saint-Honoré in 2011. The dovetailed circular space is the work of Gwenaël Nicolas, the Japan-based French architect and designer. His attention to finish is mirrored by that of Moynat's Ramesh Nair, who pored over the brand's archive to come up with the sober curves and beautiful proportions of a new line of luggage and leather goods. Moynat was a leader in automobile trunks in the 19th century, innovating from its showroom on Avenue de l'Opéra. The modern collection revisits the craftsmanship of those times: initials are handpainted by a member of the tiny team upstairs, and production takes place in a small Burgundy factory. *348 rue Saint-Honoré, 1er, T 4703 8390, www.moynat.com*

Galerie Patrick Seguin

This voluminous gallery is owned and curated by Patrick and Laurence Seguin. Remodelled in 2003 by Jean Nouvel, it's a beautifully lit space in Bastille, presenting decorative pieces and furnishings by France's most important midcentury architects and designers. Collaborations with institutions such as New York's MoMA and the Vitra Design Museum in Weil am Rhein have led to exhibitions featuring the work of perennial favourites Jean Prouvé and Charlotte Perriand, as well as Le Corbusier, Jean Royère and Pierre Jeanneret. If you're shopping properly, your pockets will need to be well lined, as these items don't come cheap. However, if you are merely browsing, you will leave this heavenly store with your imaginary modernist mansion fully furnished.
5 rue des Taillandiers, 11e, T 4700 3235, www.patrickseguin.com

L'Eclaireur

Before Colette, 10 Corso Como and Dover Street Market, there was L'Eclaireur. The original concept store, it was launched in 1980 by Armand Hadida, who, from the basement of a gallery on Champs-Élysées, became France's first distributor of such fashion designers as Martin Margiela and Ann Demeulemeester, selling them alongside a carefully edited selection of furniture. One of six L'Eclaireur stores in Paris, this branch on Rue de Sévigné was created in collaboration with conceptual artist Arne Quinze, and features a two-tonne sculpture made from wooden planks as part of an 'interactive' installation. In 2011, a Philippe Starck-designed outpost, Le Royal (T 5668 1047), was opened in the Royal Monceau hotel (see p020).
40 rue de Sévigné, 3e, T 4887 1022, www.leclaireur.com

Merci

Three decades after creating Bonpoint, the ultimate fashion destination for pint-sized patricians, Bernard and Marie-France Cohen began all over again with Merci, a concept store in Haut-Marais. Housed in an 1840 building that was once a factory for textile company Braquenié, it's a place where you can find a copy of Gide's *L'Immoraliste,* a Cappellini sofa, an Opinel pocket knife *and* a Dries Van Noten jacket. Cheap sits next to *cher*. The project is as ambitious as 10 Corso Como or The Conran Shop were back in the day, but with a difference – the profits go to charity. Order a coffee and browse the 10,000 or so secondhand titles (there's a section of English editions) in the wonderful bookshop/café (above). Closed Sundays. *111 boulevard Beaumarchais, 3ᵉ, T 4277 0033, www.merci-merci.com*

Galerie BSL

Breaking from the white-cube form, designer Noé Duchaufour-Lawrance constructed BSL's sweeping Corian spiral, which draws the eye to the products. These might include lighting by the likes of Ettore Sottsass, and jewellery by Algerian Taher Chemirik and Romanian Alina Alamorean.
23 rue Charlot, 3ᵉ, T 4478 9414, galeriebsl.com

Maison Francis Kurkdjian

In the world of perfume, Francis Kurkdjian is considered a star: he created Jean Paul Gaultier's iconic Le Mâle fragrance when he was just 25 years old, and has worked on other best-selling scents such as Elie Saab's Le Parfum. In 2009, together with business partner Marc Chaya, he launched his own-name perfume house at this bijou store situated off Rue Saint-Honoré. There are sophisticated fragrances for men and women, and all are handsomely packaged in simple bottles with zinc stoppers. If you want to create your own scent, Kurkdjian offers a bespoke service. The boutique also stocks the perfumer's range of laundry liquids, body and shower creams, scented leather bracelets and, for young noses in the making, perfumed bubbles for blowing. *5 rue d'Alger, 1er, T 4260 0707, www.franciskurkdjian.com*

Balmain

The achingly elegant and graceful flagship of the Parisian fashion house whispers chic, as you might expect from Balmain. Housed in Pierre Balmain's former design studio, founded in 1945, the first-floor boutique received a 21st-century makeover in 2009. The architect, Joseph Dirand, given free rein by the label's then creative director, Christophe Decarnin, restored the original cornicing, marble fireplaces and untreated Versailles parquet flooring to create a superlative showroom for the fashion. The furnishings demand as much attention as the clothes. Decarnin accented the space with sofas of his own design, a console by Gilbert Poillerat, a master of wrought iron, and a table by the furniture designer and sculptor André Arbus.

44 rue François, 1er, T 4720 3534,
www.balmain.com

SPORTS AND SPAS
WORK OUT, CHILL OUT OR JUST WATCH

To a large extent, Paris is not a sporting town – its gyms are dotted with the broken bodies of shocked locals who imagined that the machinery was there simply to provide a backdrop or a kind of art installation, behind, say, a cool juice bar. However, this is changing. Trickles of joggers can now be spotted in Jardin du Luxembourg, some of them putting in serious training for the Paris Marathon. Held every April, it's very nearly worth the pain because of the stunning route, beginning at the Arc de Triomphe. Even so, it is an event that most Parisians would prefer to watch rather than take to part in. And as a spectator sport it pales into insignificance compared with the epicurean pleasures to be had at the Grand Prix de Saint-Cloud and the Grand Prix de l'Arc de Triomphe – the twin pillars of Parisian horse racing.

The big crowds emerge on the third week in July, when the final stage of the Tour de France races through the city. For weeks before, the streets are full of amateurs emulating their heroes. Swimmers can make use of the art deco Piscine Pontoise-Quartier Latin (19 rue de Pontoise, 5e, T 5542 7788) and Piscine Joséphine Baker (Port de la Gare, Quai François Mauriac, 13e, T 5661 9650), a pool floating on the Seine, where you can perfect your butterfly in a structure that was conceived to make you feel as if you're in the river. And, of course, Paris boasts the chicest spas imaginable. *For full addresses, see Resources.*

Nose

Nicolas Cloutier, Romano Ricci and Marc Buxton are key members of the seven-strong team that launched 'diagnostic' perfumery Nose. Customers are quizzed about their olfactory whims before being guided towards a handful of scents that might suit. Apart from the expert staff and a sense of ceremony, albeit pretty laidback, what's on offer is a sparkling selection of brands, from Maison François Kurkdjian to Acqua di Parma and Robert Piguet's Fracas. The 175 sq m boutique, replete with fridge-style storage for the merchandise, also stocks beauty products by REN and DR Harris, and fragrance from Cire Trudon and Linari. Round the corner is the pedestrianised Rue Montorgueil, known for its delis and bakeries. *20 rue Bachaumont, 2e, T 4026 4603, www.nose.fr*

Six Senses Spa
A double-height vertical garden
designed by Patrick Blanc marks the
entrance to this centrally located spa.
Architect Pierre David filled the space
with what appear to be giant dim-sum
baskets, but which actually function as
enveloping treatment rooms, perfect
for some post-shopping R&R.
*3 rue de Castiglione, 1er, T 4316 1010,
www.sixsensesspas.com*

Klay Club

This gym was the second project from the founders of Paris' Ken Club, a trailblazer of a sports venue that raised the bar for health and fitness facilities in luxurious surroundings. Klay set new standards once again. Opened in 2009 in a former 19th-century factory, converted by the architect Cyril Durand-Behar, the 2,000 sq m space is all about industrial chic, as is evident in the pool area (above), which evokes a downtown New York hotel rather than a temple to the six-pack. The latest innovations in fitness are on the menu (the trapeze lessons devised by Cirque de Soleil have been superseded by 'Dance or Die' and TRX, inspired by American army training routines), as are developments in motivation, including a live DJ set.
4 bis, rue Saint-Sauveur, 2ᵉ, T 4026 0000, www.klay.fr

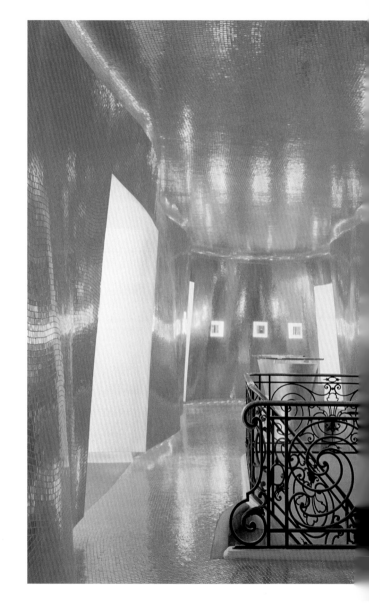

La Maison Guerlain

In 2005, architect Maxime d'Angeac and designer Andrée Putman's multimillion-euro remodelling of La Maison Guerlain reinvigorated the world's first modern beauty institute – it originally launched in 1939. With golden mosaic tiles and glass beads, the pair transformed the first floor into a scent emporium (left) and the second into a spa, offering an exceptional range of treatment programmes. While waiting in the relaxation lounge or the VIP suites on the third floor, take advantage of the view, which frames the city's busiest and still most celebrated avenue. Guerlain has been resident here for some 100 years, opening the ground-floor boutique (untouched during the renovation) in 1914, in what was originally a mansion by architect Charles Mewès, who also designed the Ritz hotel on Place Vendôme.
*68 avenue des Champs-Élysées, 8ᵉ,
T 4562 1121, www.guerlain.com*

ESCAPES

WHERE TO GO IF YOU WANT TO LEAVE TOWN

When they periodically abandon their city, where do Parisians go? The truth is, it's nowhere near Paris. If it's not Punta del Este or Sitges, it'll be the Île de Ré in Poitou-Charentes, remote Limousin, or *le Midi*. The improved scope of the TGV network means you can get to Le Havre (see p102) for an Auguste Perret architour in two hours, or to Deauville for seafood and sandy beaches in about the same time. La Grenouillère (see p100), a place of gastronomic pilgrimage, is in Montreuil-sur-Mer, just over an hour from the Gare du Nord via Rang-du-Fliers. If you're heading south, there's surely no better way to take your leave than by lingering over *un allongé* in the overblown rococo of Le Train Bleu dining room at the Gare de Lyon (1st floor, 20 boulevard Diderot, 12e, T 4343 0906).

Closer to home, the MAC/VAL museum (Place de la Libération, T 4391 6420), set in parkland in the south-eastern suburb of Vitry-sur-Seine, is a pleasant half-day diversion, or lose an afternoon in Le Pré Catelan restaurant (Route de Suresnes, 16e, T 4414 4100) in the Bois de Boulogne. Le Corbusier's exquisite Villa Savoye (see p098) is located in Poissy, to the north-west, and the stunning Hôtel du Marc (opposite) is a 45-minute train ride to the east in Reims. A two-hour drive due north, between Amiens and Lille, the Louvre-Lens museum (www.louvrelens.fr) is a new outpost of the Paris institution, designed by Japanese architects SANAA.
For full addresses, see Resources.

Hôtel du Marc, Reims

One of the most dazzling hotels in France opened in 2011, following four years of renovations to an 1840 mansion owned by Veuve Clicquot Ponsardin. A residence for the champagne house's most prestigious clients, Hôtel du Marc was reimagined by Bruno Moinard, whose restoration shows a remarkable attention to detail and a fearlessly contemporary set of interiors. The tasting room (above) features a steel and Corian table, and a neon chandelier by Jugnet + Clairet; Pablo Reinoso's work in wood writhes and curls like a *vieille vigne*; and the walls of the grand staircase are the shade of pinot noir grapes. There are five unique bedrooms; one was designed by Mathieu Lehanneur according to research into insomnia, which Madame Clicquot battled. By invitation only. *www.veuve-clicquot.com*

Villa Savoye, Poissy
Le Corbusier conceived the exemplary Villa Savoye, the purest of his purist villas, as a 'box in the air'. He used the house's structure to orchestrate the experience of entering it, as if he were directing a film. It was completed in 1931 and stands proud in a field of straggling daisies. Don't miss it. Closed Mondays.
82 rue de Villiers, T 3965 0106,
villa-savoye.monuments-nationaux.fr

La Grenouillère, Montreuil-sur-Mer
Alexandre Gauthier, chef at this family-run restaurant since 2003, found the perfect match for his culinary creativity in architect Patrick Bouchain. Beside the original farmhouse, a pair of metal 'tents' house the dining room, which is done out in wood, burlap and leather. Eight guest chalets modelled on hunting huts are tucked away in the gardens.
Rue de la Grenouillère, T 03 2106 0722

Les Bains des Docks, Le Havre
Jean Nouvel's aquatic complex, which
he called a 'universe of whiteness and
depths', makes a good diversion from a
tour of Perret's Le Havre. The modern-day
Roman bathhouse comprises 12 pools of
varying sizes, including a heated outdoor
50m pool, and facilities for balneotherapy,
children and professionals (members of
the French swimming squad train here).
Quai de la Réunion, T 02 3279 2955

NOTES

SKETCHES AND MEMOS

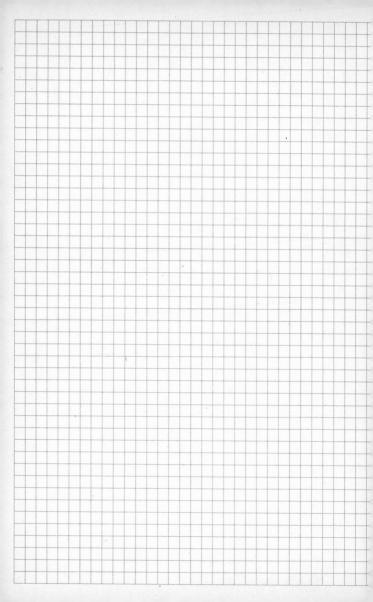

RESOURCES
CITY GUIDE DIRECTORY

A

L'Affable 062
  10 rue de Saint-Simon, 7ᵉ
  T 4222 0160
Albion 040
  80 rue du Faubourg Poissonnière, 10ᵉ
  T 4246 0244
  www.restaurantalbion.com
Apicius 048
  20 rue d'Artois, 8ᵉ
  T 4380 1966
  www.restaurant-apicius.com
L'Astrance 040
  4 rue Beethoven, 16ᵉ
  T 4050 8440
Atelier 154 076
  154 rue Oberkampf, 11ᵉ
Atelier Ozenfant 064
  53 avenue Reille, 14ᵉ
Aux Deux Amis 040
  45 rue Oberkampf, 11ᵉ
  T 5830 3813
L'Avant-Comptoir 062
  3 carrefour de l'Odéon, 6ᵉ
  T 4427 0797
Azzedine Alaïa 026
  7 rue de Moussy, 4ᵉ
  T 4272 1919

B

Les Bains des Docks 102
  Quai de la Réunion
  Le Havre
  T 02 3279 2955
  www.lesbainsdesdocks.com
Le Bal Café 042
  6 impasse de la Défense, 17ᵉ
  T 4470 7551
  www.le-bal.fr

Balades Sonores 062
  1 avenue Trudaine, 9ᵉ
  T 8387 9487
  www.baladessonores.com
Balenciaga 072
  10 avenue George V, 8ᵉ
  T 4720 2111
  www.balenciaga.com
Balmain 087
  44 rue François, 1ᵉʳ
  T 4720 3534
  www.balmain.com
Baptiste Pitou 078
  Hermès Sèvres
  17 rue de Sèvres, 6ᵉ
  T 4284 1908
Bar de la Croix Rouge 062
  2 carrefour de la Croix Rouge, 6ᵉ
  T 4548 0645
Le Baron 040
  6 avenue Marceau, 8ᵉ
  www.clublebaron.com
Le Baron Rouge 032
  1 rue Théophile Roussel, 12ᵉ
  T 4343 1432
Beef Club 060
  58 rue Jean-Jacques Rousseau, 1ᵉʳ
  T 954 371 365
  www.eccbeefclub.com
Bellota-Bellota 032
  18 rue Jean-Nicot, 7ᵉ
  T 5359 9696
  www.bellota-bellota.com
Le Bon Marché Rive Gauche 073
  24 rue de Sèvres, 7ᵉ
  T 4439 8000
  www.lebonmarche.com

HOTELS
ADDRESSES AND ROOM RATES

Auberge Flora 016
  Room rates:
  double, from €90
  44 boulevard Richard-Lenior, 11ᵉ
  T 4700 5277
  www.aubergeflora.fr

Le Citizen Hôtel 022
  Room rates:
  double, from €195;
  Zen Suite 66, from €275
  96 quai de Jemmapes, 10ᵉ
  T 8362 5550
  www.lecitizenhotel.com

Crayon Hôtel 016
  Room rates:
  double, from €150
  25 rue du Bouloi, 1ᵉʳ
  T 4236 5419
  www.hotelcrayon.com

La Grenouillère 100
  Room rates:
  double, from €140;
  Huttes, €215
  Rue de la Grenouillère
  Montreuil-sur-Mer
  T 03 2106 0722
  www.lagrenouillere.fr

Hôtel Jules et Jim 027
  Room rates:
  double, from €200
  11 rue des Gravilliers, 3ᵉ
  T 4454 1313
  www.hoteljulesetjim.com

La Maison Champs Élysées 018
  Room rates:
  double, from €300;
  Suite, from €350;
  Suite Salon Doré, €1,250
  8 rue Jean Goujon, 8ᵉ
  T 4074 6465
  www.lamaisonchampselysees.com

Mama Shelter 028
  Room rates:
  double, from €90;
  Room 526, €90
  109 rue de Bagnolet, 20ᵉ
  T 4348 4848
  www.mamashelter.com

Mandarin Oriental 016
  Room rates:
  double, from €795
  247-251 rue Saint-Honoré, 1ᵉʳ
  T 7098 7888
  www.mandarinoriental.com

Hôtel du Marc 097
  By invitation only
  Reims
  www.veuve-clicquot.com

Hôtel Particulier Montmartre 030
  Room rates:
  double, from €390;
  Poèmes et Chapeaux Suite, €490;
  Rideau de Cheveux Suite, €590
  23 avenue Junot, 18ᵉ
  T 5341 8140
  www.hotel-particulier-montmartre.com

Le Pavillon de la Reine 024
Room rates:
double, from €390;
Superior Room, €460;
Suite de la Reine, €950
28 place des Vosges, 3ᵉ
T 4029 1919
www.pavillon-de-la-reine.com

The Peninsula 016
Room rates:
prices on request
19 avenue Kléber
www.peninsula.com

La Réserve 017
Rates:
Apartment 5, from €2,800;
Apartment 3, from €3,300;
Apartment 1, from €4,300
10 place du Trocadéro, 16ᵉ
T 5370 5370
www.lareserve-paris.com

Le Royal Monceau 020
Room rates:
double, from €850;
Gallery Suite, from €1,850
37 avenue Hoche, 8ᵉ
T 4299 8800
www.leroyalmonceau.com

3 Rooms 026
Rates:
One-bedroom apartment, from €450
5 rue de Moussy, 4ᵉ
T 4478 9200

Hôtel Thoumieux 021
Room rates:
double, from €150;
Junior Suite, €320
79 rue Saint-Dominique, 7ᵉ
T 4705 4975
www.thoumieux.fr

W Paris Opéra 016
Room rates:
double, €590
4 rue Meyerbeer, 9ᵉ
T 7748 9494
www.wparisopera.com

WALLPAPER* CITY GUIDES

Executive Editor
Rachael Moloney

Author
Sophie Dening

Art Director
Loran Stosskopf
Art Editor
Eriko Shimazaki
Designer
Mayumi Hashimoto
Map Illustrator
Russell Bell

Photography Editor
Sophie Corben
Acting Photography Editor
Elisa Merlo
Photography Assistant
Nabil Butt

Chief Sub-Editor
Nick Mee
Sub-Editor
Julia Chadwick

Editorial Assistant
Emma Harrison

Interns
Nathalie Akkaoui
Thomas Atkins
Laura Font Sentis
Asha Aarti Mistry

Wallpaper* Group Editor-in-Chief
Tony Chambers
Publishing Director
Gord Ray
Managing Editor
Jessica Diamond
Acting Managing Editor
Oliver Adamson

Contributors
Greg Foster
Amy Serafin

Wallpaper* ® is a registered trademark of IPC Media Limited

First published 2006
Revised and updated
2008, 2009, 2010, 2011
and 2013

© 2006, 2008, 2009,
2010, 2011 and 2013
IPC Media Limited

ISBN 978 0 7148 6458 7

All prices are correct at
the time of going to press,
but are subject to change.

Printed in China

PHAIDON

Phaidon Press Limited
Regent's Wharf
All Saints Street
London N1 9PA

Phaidon Press Inc
180 Varick Street
New York, NY 10014

Phaidon® is a registered
trademark of Phaidon
Press Limited

www.phaidon.com

A CIP Catalogue record for
this book is available from
the British Library.

PHOTOGRAPHERS

Corbis
Paris city view,
inside front cover

Michel Denancé
Hermès Sèvres, p078

Adrien Dirand
Balmain, p087

Eric Forlini
En Selle Marcel, p074

Clément Guillaume
La Maison Champs
Élysées, pp018-019
Le Royal Monceau, p020
Hôtel Thoumieux, p021
Pâtisserie des
Martyrs, p033
Galerie Kreo, pp036-037
Septime, p038, p039
L'Opéra, p041
Le Bal Café, pp042-043
L'Office, p044, p045
Compagnie des Vins
Surnaturels, pp046-047
Sur Mesure par Thierry
Marx, pp050-051
Le 39V, p052
Le Dauphin, pp054-055
Saturne, p059
Julie Rousselet, p063
Communist Party
Headquarters, pp068-069
Nose, p089
Les Bains des Docks,
pp102-103

Alexandre Guirkinger
Moynat, p079
Merci, p083

Alex Hill
Mama Shelter, pp028-029
Hôtel Particulier, p031
Musée du quai
Branly, p035

Hotelexistence.com
Grande Arche de la
Défense, p011
UNESCO Headquarters,
pp012-013
Maison de Verre, p065

**Hotelexistence.com
(FLC/ADAGP, Paris and
DACS London 2012)**
Villa Savoye, pp098-099

**Jakob + MacFarlane/
N Borel Photography**
Cité de la Mode et du
Design, pp066-067

**Jean-Noël
Leblanc-Bontemps**
Boulogne-Billancourt,
pp070-071
La Maison Guerlain,
pp094-095

Florent Michel
Palais de Tokyo, p034

Kristen Pelou
Beef Club, pp060-061

Ildiko Peter
La Grenouillère, pp100-101

Gaële Pierre
Le Citizen Hotel, pp022-023

Mario Pignata Monti
Le 39V, p053

James Reeve
Le Pavillon de la Reine,
p024, p025
Hôtel Particulier, p030
Brasserie Thoumieux,
pp056-057
Frenchie, p058
Naço Gallery, p075
Atelier 154, pp076-077
L'Eclaireur, p082
Maison Francis
Kurkdjian, p086

Philippe Schaff
Apicius, p048

**Courtesy of Patrick
Seguin Gallery**
Galerie Patrick Seguin,
pp080-081

Sebastien Veronese
Hôtel Jules et Jim, p027

PARIS
A COLOUR-CODED GUIDE TO THE CITY'S HOT 'HOODS

MONTMARTRE
Up the hill is home to the *haute bourgeoisie*; at its foot is the city's (reformed) sin central

CANAL SAINT-MARTIN
Alongside this canal in the 10th arrondissement, east-Paris bobos set up shop and play

CHAMPS-ÉLYSÉES
Les Champs will always be touristy, but the area around it is full of stylish destinations

RÉPUBLIQUE/BASTILLE
More polished these days, thanks to a shot of *bon chic, bon genre*. Eat on Rue Paul Bert

MARAIS
These streets were made for strolling. Galleries, boutiques, bars, bistros – take your pick

BEAUBOURG/LOUVRE
Come here for art and architecture that is impossible to miss and still able to inspire

SAINT-GERMAIN DES-PRÉS/QUARTIER LATIN
Sartre and de Beauvoir's Left Bank stomping ground is more about shopping these days

LES INVALIDES
The monumental heart of the city now has another prize – Jean Nouvel's museum

For a full description of each neighbourhood, see the Introduction.
Featured venues are colour-coded, according to the district in which they are located.